D1557018

SEEDS OF FAITH

Joy

SEEDS OF FAITH

Joy

Words of Faith from
NORMAN VINCENT PEALE

Ideals Publications · Nashville, Tennessee

ISBN 0-8249-4642-1

Published by Ideals Publications, a division of Guideposts
535 Metroplex Drive, Suite 250, Nashville, Tennessee 37211
www.idealsbooks.com

Editor, Peggy Schaefer
Designer, Marisa Calvin
Cover photograph: Index Stock/Alamy Images

Printed and bound in Mexico by RR Donnelley
10 9 8 7 6 5 4 3 2 1

ACKNOWLEDGMENTS
All scripture quotations, unless otherwise noted, are taken from
The King James Version of the Bible.

Joy increases as you give it.
In giving it, you will accumulate
a deposit of joy greater than
you ever believed possible.

—NORMAN VINCENT PEALE

FOREWORD

Throughout his long career, my father, Norman Vincent Peale, valued no message more than that of the importance of faith in each of our lives. In fact, before the title was finalized, *The Power of Positive Thinking* was called *The Power of Faith*. It was that important to him.

Growing up in the Midwest at the beginning of the twentieth century, Dad learned about faith at his parents' knees and in the pews of small-town churches. Faith in God, country, and fellow man, and the saving message of Jesus Christ filled his youthful days. He learned oratorical skills by listening to the great preachers of the day,

who went from town to town, bringing countless people to faith. He became filled with faith messages, and they never left him.

When the personal call came for him to enter the ministry, Dad was well equipped with deep faith, a gift for communicating, and a love of people. His writings were full of anecdotes of the faith journeys of countless people he met along the way. By their examples, he was able to lead others to a life of faith. His was a great calling, and I think we can all agree that he succeeded.

As you read, I hope you enjoy the messages in this book and that it brings deeper faith into your life.

—*Elizabeth Peale Allen*

These **things** have I spoken *unto* **you,** that my **joy** might **remain** in you, and that **your joy** might be **full.** —John 15:11

he Christian faith is the Gospel of joy and happiness, for even in the midst of the pain, difficulty, and sorrow we encounter in life, the Bible teaches us to be happy. It is full of statements about joy and happiness. Your guide to happiness is Christ—and His way of life. His teachings make us happy, radiant, joyful, successful.

Jesus makes us glad. He makes us sing.

Do you want it—this life of joy and happiness? You must surrender your whole self to God through Jesus Christ. Pray for it, act on it, believe it, and you will begin at once to feel His power in you. Plant this idea firmly in your mind, affirm it every day, strive for it. Try to make yourself worthy of being a temple for His Spirit. There is not a soul upon earth who cannot make his or her life a marvelous thing, a tremendous and joyous experience.

Think about the promise, "What things soever ye desire, when ye pray, believe that ye receive them, and ye shall have them" (Mark 11:24). What a marvelous promise this is, and how true you can prove it to be!

Minister and author Stanley Jones said that it is much more fun being a Christian than going to the devil. One feeds a life, the other satisfies an impulse. One ends in a mess, the other in the joy of living. Many things will happen to you when you take Jesus Christ as your guide to happiness. Many little coincidences will take place in your daily life which you had previously looked upon as good luck. But they are all part of that divine plan, for the world is created by a God who runs it on laws; and when you live up to those laws, then the joy of living becomes a daily coincidence for you.

Who decides whether you shall be happy or unhappy? You do!

A television celebrity host had as a guest on his program an aged man. And he was a rare old man indeed. His remarks were entirely unpremeditated. They simply bubbled up out of a personality that was radiant and happy. And whenever he said anything, it was so naive, so apt, that the audience roared with laughter. They loved him. Impressed, the celebrity host enjoyed the experience along with his audience.

Finally he asked the old man why he was so happy. "You must have a wonderful secret of happiness," he suggested.

"No," replied the old man, "I haven't any great secret. It's just as plain as the nose on your face. When I get up in the morning I have two choices—to be happy or unhappy. I just choose to be happy."

You can be unhappy if you want to be. It is the easiest thing in the world to accomplish. Just choose unhappiness. Go around telling yourself that things aren't going well, that nothing is satisfactory, and you can be quite sure of being unhappy. But say to

This is the day
which the LORD hath made;
we will rejoice and be glad in it.

PSALM 118:24

yourself, "Things are going nicely. Life is good. I choose happiness," and you can be quite certain of having your choice.

Many of us manufacture our own unhappiness. Of course not all unhappiness is self-created, for social conditions are responsible for not a few of our woes. Yet, to a large extent, by our thoughts and attitudes we distill out of the ingredients of life either happiness or unhappiness for ourselves. Anyone who desires it, who wills it, and who learns and applies the right formula may become a happy person.

Tomorrow when you arise, say out loud three

times this one sentence, "This is the day which the LORD hath made; we will rejoice and be glad in it" (Psalm 118:24). Only personalize it and say, "I will rejoice and be glad in it." Repeat it in a strong, clear voice and with positive tone and emphasis.

While dressing or getting breakfast, say aloud a few such remarks as, "I believe I can successfully handle all problems that will arise today. I feel good physically, mentally, emotionally. It is wonderful to be alive. I am grateful for all that I have had, for all that I now have, and for all that I shall have. Things aren't going to fall apart. God is here and He is with me and He will see me through. I thank God for every good thing." Throughout the day, base your actions and attitudes upon fundamental principles of happy living.

One of the simplest and most basic of such principles is that of human love and goodwill. It is amazing what happiness a sincere expression of compassion and tenderness will induce.

A friend of mine, H. C. Mattern, is a genuinely happy man who, with his equally happy wife, Mary, travels throughout the country. Mr. Mattern carries a unique business card on the reverse side of which is printed the philosophy which has brought happiness to him and his wife and to hundreds of others who have been so fortunate as to feel the impact of their personalities.

The card reads: "The way to happiness: keep your heart free from hate, your mind from worry. Live simply, expect little, give much. Fill your life with love. Scatter sunshine. Forget self, think of others. Do as you would be done by. Try this for a week and you will be surprised."

As you read these words, you may say, "There is nothing new in that." Indeed, there is something new in it if you have never tried it. When you start to practice it, you will find it the most astonishing method of happy and successful living you have ever used.

A thing of beauty is a joy forever; its loveliness increases; it will never pass into nothingness.

JOHN KEATS

Of course, in order to give power to these principles of happiness and make them work, it is necessary to support them with a dynamic quality of mind. You are not likely to secure effective results even with spiritual principles without spiritual power. When one experiences a dynamic spiritual change inwardly, success with happiness-producing ideas becomes extraordinarily easy. If you begin to use spiritual principles, however awkwardly, you will gradually experience spiritual power inwardly. This will give you the greatest surge of happiness you have ever known. It will stay with you as long as you live a God-centered life.

We live in a time of great affluence. But seemingly there are more emotionally and mentally miserable people in the United States than we have ever previously had.

What's come over us? What's gone wrong with us? We need a new philosophy of optimism. Let us get rid of this gloom and depressiveness in the name of the only one who can lift the shadows and let in the sunlight, namely, Jesus Christ our Lord.

When a young friend of mine heard that I was going to talk on the powerful effect of optimism, he berated me. "In the first place," he said, "optimism is silly. And in the second place, if you want to find optimism, the church isn't the place to find it." He then described the many dull, sleepy and (to use his words) dopey preachments he had heard in church. When I pressed him, I found he hadn't been to church in a while, but still he had an image of tediously dull sermons.

I said to my friend "You seem to have a tired view of life. You're so sad always. Why are you so sad?"

"Because life is sad," he replied.

Well, life does have plenty of trouble in it. It is

full of deep, grievous trouble. And Christianity recognizes this. The reason Christianity survives is that it faces all aspects of life, including all the evil thereof and all the wickedness in man. It paints the whole picture but, nevertheless, affirms that in the midst of all this trouble, pain, and confusion, there is a good outcome—a lilting something that sings its way out of sorrow.

Optimism, hope, freshness, newness. One Bible text after another speaks to us of these: "If any man be in Christ, he is a new creature: old things are passed away; behold, all things are become new" (2 Corinthians 5:17). Again: ". . . walk in newness of life"

(Romans 6:4). And again: "I saw a new heaven and a new earth: for the first heaven and the first earth were passed away" (Revelation 21:1). Freshness, newness—this is Christianity in its essence.

And what is optimism? Well, before we answer that question, let us ask, "What is pessimism?" Pessimism is a philosophy that holds that the evil in life overbalances the good in life.

Optimism, on the other hand, is a philosophy based on the belief that, basically, life is good, created and sustained by a good God. And that, in the long run, the good in life overbalances the evil. Also that in every difficulty and every pain, there is some inherent good. And the optimist means to find that good.

Optimism isn't some cheery, Cheshire-cat, moonlight-and-roses philosophy at all. To be a true optimist, you must be rugged and tough in mind. No soft person can be an optimist. An optimist is a person who believes in a good outcome, even when he can't yet see it. He is a person who believes in a greater day, when there is no evidence of it. He is one who believes in his own future, even when he can't see much possibility in it.

"Well," you say, "I'd like to be optimistic, but I have a lot of dark clouds in my mind all the time. I

A joyful
heart is the
inevitable result
of a heart
burning with love.
MOTHER TERESA

see nothing but the gloom and the hardship and the pain and the suffering. It's all very well for you to talk so enthusiastically, but what am I going to do with all these clouds? I have a low ceiling."

Many people do live under a low ceiling. Why not go out and take a few plane rides and see what a low ceiling really amounts to? Up above the clouds, the sun is always shining. Down here, on earth's surface, groping around in the shadows under a low ceiling, a person may not feel optimistic. But you should begin to practice the optimistic upthrust. Send up into the mass of dark clouds bright, power- ful, optimistic thoughts and optimistic faith. By doing so, you can dissipate the clouds and have an entirely different life. Send up constantly into the overcast shrouding your mind bright thoughts of faith, love, and hope; thoughts of God; thoughts about the wonderful greatness of life.

The poet Walt Whitman wrote, "To me every hour of the light and dark is a miracle." The author Robert Louis Stevenson wrote, "To miss the joy is to miss all." The poet Edna St. Vincent Millay exclaimed, "O world, I cannot hold thee close enough!" Paul Tillich, a theologian, tells us, "Where there is joy, there is fulfillment, and where there is fulfillment, there is joy."

Optimism, when it is applied to our lives, cleanses the mind of unhealthy thoughts. And, of course, unhealthy thoughts quickly take away the joy, the peace, and even the health of life. An injection of Christian optimism will rejuvenate the entire social order.

So let go of that gloom, let go of that depression, let go of that discouragement, let go of that weakness, let go of that sense of failure. Get yourself with Jesus—really, personally. Go to Him, pray to Him, tell Him you want to live with Him, tell Him you want to be guided in your life by Him.

And I will guarantee, on the basis of everything I have seen in my ministry, that you will become optimistic; you will become victorious; you will have peace in your heart; you will love people; you will feel good physically and emotionally. You will have a wonderful life.

There's no danger of developing eyestrain from looking on the bright side.

*G*od loves you so much that He is interested deeply in you and all your concerns. So when you are troubled or discouraged or maybe frightened, all you

For the heart
that finds joy in
small things, in all things,
each day is a
wonderful gift.
ANGELUS
SILESIUS

have to do is talk to Him. He is always listening, always eager to help.

But some people, while they believe in God, find it difficult to reach Him. He seems just too far off.

To one man who expressed such a feeling I told a simple story about an economist who, years ago, wanted to reach the late Wendell Wilkie, then a presidential candidate. He wanted Mr. Wilkie to write the foreword for a book he had written. He hunted about among his friends, trying to find someone through whom he could meet Mr. Wilkie. Finally he found a man who had worked at one time in Mr. Wilkie's office.

"Mr. Wilkie is a very important man," he hedged. "If you will give me a week or two, I will see if I can make some connection by which you might meet him."

So the economist tried another gentleman, who said, "I think if I have lunch with so-and-so, he might introduce me. Then we could see about making the contact."

But the economist had a secretary who was a smart woman. "There is a telephone here," she said, "and there is a telephone in Mr. Wilkie's office. Why don't you call him?"

"He will be surrounded with secretaries."

"All they can say is 'no.' Try it," she counseled.

The economist did. "I wonder if you would give a message to Mr. Wilkie," he began. "Some time when he has two minutes free, I would like to present a matter to him."

"I'm free now," said the answering voice on the telephone. "This is Wendell Wilkie. Tell me what you want."

This is a basic way to get results. If you want something from Almighty God, if you need help, simply ask Him; and believe that you are going to get an answer and the help you need.

When you ask in this simple and direct manner,

also ask in a big and expectant manner. Many of us fail because we pray such little prayers. I do not claim to be an authority on how God reacts, but I wonder if He pays much attention to little prayers, because a little prayer indicates a lack of faith. Pray big prayers with deep and genuine belief, even if your problem seems small and routine. The Lord is very generous.

Children know by nature how to be happy. The world is fresh and wonderful to them. The simplest, most commonplace things are endowed with romance; and a child has the time of his life just living. It is the great simplicities of life, not the complexities, not the sophistications, that produce happiness.

I am reminded of an experience with my daughter Elizabeth when she was nine years old. I asked her, "Are you happy, honey?"

"Sure I'm happy," she replied.

"Are you always happy? Is there a time when you're unhappy?" I persisted.

"No, Daddy," she assured me.

"That's wonderful. What makes you happy?"

"My playmates make me happy; I like them.

Hitherto have ye asked nothing in my name: ask, and ye shall receive, that your joy may be full.

JOHN 16:24

My school makes me happy; I like to go to school. I like to go to church and Sunday school. I like my mother and father. They take care of me when I'm sick, and they love me and are good to me."

In thinking about her answer, I realized it is all there. Her playmates—that is, her associates; her school—that is, where she works; her church and Sunday school—that is, where she worships; her mother and father—that is, the home circle where protection and love are. Happiness lies in basic and simple things, not in something artificial like radios, television, automobiles, or lots of such things. Children understand intuitively where happiness is.

According to a newspaper report, a number of boys and girls were asked to list things that made them happiest. Here is what the boys listed: a swallow flying; looking into deep, clear water; the furrow of the water cut by the bow of a boat; a fast train rushing by; a builder's crane lifting a heavy load; a dog's eyes.

Here is what the girls said made them happy: street lights on the river; red roofs against the trees; smoke rising from a chimney; red velvet; the moon in the clouds.

You see, to be truly happy you must want to be happy. Do not fool yourself. Begin each day by saying aloud, "I am happy." Then act happy. Practice affirming happiness, which is a positive attitude of mind. In so doing, you will condition yourself to affirm faith. And strong affirmation of faith is an essential ingredient of happiness.

Along with affirmation, use visualization or imaging. Believe so strongly that you picture amazing blessings from God. This process, taken all together, is one of the surest ways to a deep and unbroken happiness.

Never let trouble, no matter how devastating it may appear to be, take charge of your thoughts and determine your attitude. Always affirm the best, believe in the best, image the best, pray for the best; and the strong tendency will be for the best to come to you. This is the chief guarantee of happiness.

While we are considering the joy of a positive attitude, it may also be well to think of the contrary attitude of unhappiness. The famous writer and psychologist William James said:

"The attitude of unhappiness is not only painful, it is also mean and ugly. What can be more base and unworthy than the pining, puling, mumping mood, no matter by what outward ills it may have been engendered? What is more injurious to others? What less helpful as a way out of difficulty? It but fastens and perpetuates the trouble which occasioned it. . . ."

Life is the most marvelous tool God has created for you. Everything on earth has been put here at man's disposal. God intends for you to use life. He wants you to take advantage of all the things He has put here, and to use them as resources and opportunities.

When you arise in the morning, form a resolution to make the day a happy one for a fellow creature.

*Joy is
magnified when shared.*

TIM HANSEL

Never give way to melancholy; resist it steadily, for the habit will encroach. A positive attitude that is joyful and enthusiastic will, if sincerely and long held, produce joyful, enthusiastic and positive results in our lives. If we hold negative thoughts until they dominate our minds, if we look for sin and sickness in everyone, we will certainly find it.

Every day can be a blue day to you, every night just another night of misery. You produce in your daily life these very things by constantly impressing wrong ideas upon your mind. Every person living on this earth is as he is because of the pattern of his past thinking, and if your life has been unhappy up to now, then it is time for you to change your ideas and begin to practice a Christianity that will radiate happy living into your experiences.

Many of you enjoyed, no doubt, during the last summer, a wonderful vacation, going to new places, seeing new areas, meeting different people who are all living very different lives from your own. You came back with a thoroughly different picture of life from that you had before. You came home refreshed, after being absent for some time from your daily toil, your daily worries, the people who annoyed you. Oh, how much you enjoyed the change. You lived happily during your vacation.

Was it a miserable world to you then? Did you not enjoy every minute of it? Did you not love the beauties of the sea, the forest, the country-side, the lakeshore? Was it a hell on earth to you or was it a picture of God's perfection? You had a complete change of scene and peace of mind. In those few weeks you changed the pattern of your thinking, and what did you find? In the beauties of nature you found God and you found a heaven on earth. You loved life while on your vacation, didn't you? Then why is it not possible to enjoy this happy living 365 days a year?

The Bible says, "He that will love life and see good days," and this tells you very definitely that the Master, Jesus Christ, knows all about life, knows all about the good in life, all about good living, and He wants you, as a child of His Father, to share that good life, to be happy with Him right now.

You can make your life a happy one if, first of all, you will forget and forgive the past, if you will learn to live one day at a time, believing that a radiant future is yours.